The
CONVERSATION BLUEPRINT

*Building Relationships
One Great Conversation at a Time*

Tad Dwyer, M.Ed.

The Conversation Blueprint

Building Relationships One Great Conversation at a Time

Tad Dwyer, M.Ed.

ISBN (Print Edition): 978-1-66787-664-1

ISBN (eBook Edition): 978-1-66787-665-8

© 2022. All rights reserved. No part of this publication may be reproduced, distributed, or transmitted in any form or by any means, including photocopying, recording, or other electronic or mechanical methods, without the prior written permission of the publisher, except in the case of brief quotations embodied in critical reviews and certain other noncommercial uses permitted by copyright law.

*To my wife Tammy and my children Brandon and Nicholas,
who remind me every day that life is far
too precious to be a bystander.*

CONTENTS

Introduction *Great Conversations* — 1

Chapter 1 *The Challenge* — 3

Chapter 2 *The Consultant (and Sister!)* — 7

Chapter 3 *A Way Forward* — 9

Chapter 4 *Pre-Work* — 13

Chapter 5 *Debrief* — 17

Chapter 6 *Groundwork* — 21

Chapter 7 *Conversation Plan* — 35

Chapter 8 *Post-Work* — 45

Chapter 9 *TCB with Colleagues* — 47

Chapter 10 *TCB with Your Direct Leader* — 53

Chapter 11 *TCB with Sr. Leaders (C-Suite)* — 59

Chapter 12 *TCB with Direct Reports* — 63

Chapter 13 *1+1 and Putting It All Together* — 67

Chapter 14 *TCB with Difficult Colleagues* — 75

Chapter 15 *New Build's New Sr. Leader* — 79

Epilogue *Putting TCB into Practice* — 81

Acknowledgements — 83

About the Author — 85

INTRODUCTION

Great Conversations

Great, career-defining work relationships do not happen by accident. They happen one conversation and interaction at a time. Working with talented leaders to better frame their conversations is a gift, and it's one of the many things I love about being an Organization Development Consultant and coach. This work led me to design The Conversation Blueprint™ ("TCB") framework featured throughout this book. I created TCB so that leaders at all levels could have a way to plan for and attain great conversations—and prevent regrettable ones.

I know I'm not alone when I say that I have a few relationships that are weaker than they could be, due to one or two conversations that went poorly. This was particularly true when I was surprised by the conversation topic, or its intensity. I wish I had those conversations back. If I did have them to do over again, I would be more deliberate and give thought to what I wanted to accomplish before the interactions, rather than just letting them happen to me and reacting.

This book summarizes the leadership journey of Alia Davis, a gifted subject matter expert who wants more out of her current job. By working with her sister Whitney (an OD consultant), Alia learns to apply The Conversation Blueprint to improve her current relationships and build new ones.

THE CONVERSATION BLUEPRINT

If you hold a role in any organization, the ensuing story should resonate well for you. Our organizations are far more fluid and freer flowing now than at any time in history. Technology and the knowledge-work revolution mean that we interact with a greater variety of people at all levels in our organizations than our predecessors ever did. In a single day, you could field inquiries from your boss, colleagues, direct reports, and members of senior leadership, including those in high ranking executive or "chief" positions, also called the "C-suite." The situations we face today are also varied and unpredictable, leading many of my clients to say, "You couldn't make up the situation I had to deal with today." Some of the many situations I've heard about include:

- "Due to a corporate restructuring, a very close friend outside of work, whom I recommended for a job at my company in a different department, will now be reporting directly to me."

- "The CFO at my firm is making 'suggestions' to me, an individual contributor, about sales materials I'm responsible for developing, and then following up to see if they've been done, without even talking to my boss!"

- "Our company is under new ownership and the demands on my boss have obviously intensified, but it is nothing that we've discussed openly."

The Conversation Blueprint is designed to help identify the different factors that impact our ability to have great conversations, plan for them, and then lay the groundwork to be our best selves when engaging in those conversations.

The book is divided into two sections. The first section (Chapters 1-8) explains The Conversation Blueprint process, while the second section (Chapters 9-15) shows the process in action, as well as providing tips, tools, and practices to use in several different situations.

Have fun reading the story, identifying similar situations you've been in, and imagining many great conversations to come.

CHAPTER 1
The Challenge

Alia Davis arrived at her office later than usual on Monday morning. She was still upset about hearing the news that she had been passed over for a promotion late last week. Her boss, Shayla Maye, informed Alia of the decision, but the two still have not had a chance to discuss the situation in detail. While the person promoted does not report to Shayla, Alia knows that her boss can provide her with more information than she currently has.

Alia is the Digital Marketing Manager at NewBuild, a company providing commercial building infrastructure services. Since joining NewBuild just over four years ago, she has enjoyed a steady stream of praise for her ability to create an industry-best web presence. NewBuild has been growing steadily ever since Alia was recruited to join the firm by her close friend, Cody Wilkes, the company's Director of Online Sales. Over the last year, however, NewBuild has accelerated its acquisitions (as well as revenue streams and clients) by purchasing several boutique firms. NewBuild has also benefitted from increased sales in its core business, due in large part to brand popularity and the online presence that Alia and her team so proudly built.

Although Alia was trying not to think any more about the promotion and focus on the long list of important deliverables in front of her, she was still upset about the news. As a result, she was having a hard time concentrating. As she went through her e-mails and voicemails, Alia began to feel even more deflated. The number of requests she receives daily have steadily increased over the past few months, including from NewBuild employees she hasn't even met yet.

Just then, Alia was joined in her office by Shayla, who asked if Alia had a few minutes to talk. Alia said she did, and Shayla took a seat next to Alia. Alia knew that Shayla had her own issues to deal with, particularly adjusting to a demanding new boss who joined the company just two months ago. "I know you're disappointed about not getting the Program Manager position, Alia, and I want to talk with you about that and answer any questions that I can."

"I appreciate that, Shayla," Alia replied. "You're right, I am disappointed, and I appreciate your coming by. I know it was a sought-after position, but it stings that it went to someone else, particularly someone with less time at the company than me."

"I know, Alia. I hope you know that I advocated for you. I did. I also understand why the company chose the candidate they did."

"Okay, let's start there. Why was the other candidate chosen?" Alia asked, a bit defensively.

"While you both have outstanding project management and technical backgrounds, the other candidate has an extensive network inside and outside the organization. The company thought this would help them be successful in the PM role," Shayla told Alia as gently as she could.

"So, if I hear you right, the other candidate is more outgoing and that was the difference in the decision?" Alia asked.

"Your reputation here is stellar, Alia. The senior team was insistent that I talk with you to let you know that. And, no it wasn't because the other candidate is more outgoing. To be honest they are pretty shy. It's the quality of the network they have."

"I'm confused by that Shayla. I really am."

"Do you remember the company wide 360 initiative that we engaged in last year?" Shayla asked.

"I do," Alia replied sheepishly, as she suddenly had a pretty good idea what her boss was referring to.

"I think your areas needing development, particularly around reacting to changes effectively and building deep relationships with those outside your team, are things you and I should work on more together. In fact, I take responsibility for not making more time to work with you personally on these things, Alia. I promise to be better in the future."

"This is not on you, Shayla. I'll take you up on working more closely with me on this though. The truth is, I got that feedback a while ago and haven't done that much with it, given all we've got on our plates. I don't mean that as an excuse. I get it. I appreciate your coming by, Shayla, and I'll get over it," Alia assured her boss.

"I don't want you to get over it, Alia! I want you to get the next promotion that's available here. We're growing by leaps and bounds and you're too good not to get the next one," Shayla assured her.

"Thanks Shayla. I appreciate your coming by first thing today."

With that, Shayla and Alia concluded their conversation. After Shayla left, Alia knew what she had to do. It was time to reach out to Whitney, Alia's sister and "secret weapon."

CHAPTER 2
The Consultant (and Sister!)

Whitney Davis-Parker is an independent Organization Development consultant, and the proud big sister of Alia Davis. Whitney began her career as a trainer and course designer for a local community bank. She loved the work and the people and was devastated when the bank was acquired by a large national bank.

She stayed with the larger entity for a year before deciding to leave and join a start-up with colleagues she met in graduate school. As the organization grew, she held leadership positions in operations and human capital and eventually became the Vice President of Organizational Learning and Development.

These experiences, as well as teaching at her alma mater, gave her the confidence to open her own consulting practice with a focus on executive coaching and leadership development. Early in her practice, a close friend (who is also a brilliant executive and partner in a private equity firm) engaged Whitney to consult with her company to help in the development of their portfolio companies and executives. This gave Whitney the opportunity to hone her skills in a lightning-fast "meritocracy" where results are demanded.

Whitney has watched her sister succeed in her career and has been her number one supporter. She has provided Alia with help and advice over the years and always looks forward to the opportunity to talk with her for any reason. As such, she was thrilled to receive a lunch invitation from her sister today, particularly since Pomegranate Tikka Masala is on the menu of their favorite restaurant.

CHAPTER 3
A Way Forward

At lunch, the two sisters got right to business, as was their norm. Whitney updated Alia on her latest projects, and Alia brought Whitney up to speed on how she had been feeling lately about work.

Alia told her sister, "I'm feeling disappointed and overwhelmed lately as well."

"Disappointed?" Whitney asked.

"You know my interest in learning new things and growing," Alia said.

"Well, learning new things has always been a fascination—forget that—an addiction for you," Whitney replied.

Alia laughed. "I suppose that's fair. And I recently found out I was passed over for a promotion I really wanted that would have allowed me to learn a ton about the business and our operations. In my current role, I'm getting fewer opportunities to learn and am spending way more time just, well, reacting."

"I'm sorry to hear about the promotion, Alia."

"Well, that's a big reason I wanted to talk with you Whit," Alia continued. "That and constant reacting has me enjoying my job less and less lately."

"Got it. That makes sense. What does reacting look and feel like in your world?" Whitney asked.

"Constant interruptions. Be it from e-mail, people stopping by, texting, phone, you name it."

"Have these interruptions increased more lately?" Whitney wondered.

"Oh yeah! Sometimes new colleagues introduce themselves to me and ask for something in the same breath! And I've found myself doing the same thing," Alia admitted.

Whitney nodded understandingly as her sister continued. "Especially given my role as webmaster. I'm one of the first people brought into newly acquired companies to understand their product lines and services. When new companies come into the fold via acquisition, my workload increases dramatically, and NewBuild is in 'buy mode.' The worst part, though, is that I don't feel connected to my colleagues anymore. You know me; I'm not that outgoing, especially with people I don't know well. I don't want to not know who I'm working with, or whether my input is helping or not." Alia paused to reflect for a moment and then continued. "I could blame my not getting the promotion on the increased workload and lack of time. I also have no use for 'self-promotion,' however NewBuild has an excellent track record of promoting based on merit and fit for the next job. I know that there's something missing in 'my game' to get to the next level. My most recent 360 review listed building deep relationships outside my team and handling changes effectively as developmental opportunities. While I believe this to be true, I really don't know how to go about improving in these areas. Ultimately, that, dear sister, is why I called you."

Whitney responded to her sister, "This reminds me of so many conversations I've had with my clients. You are not alone; I assure you of that, Alia. I have an idea. I am doing a favor for a colleague and have agreed to teach a module on a framework I call "The Conversation Blueprint" as part of her Leadership Development course at the community college next Saturday. I am sure she wouldn't mind if you joined us then. There is a pre-class assignment. If you're willing to do that, you would be ready for the class. What do you say?"

"Seriously, Whit? That would be great. I'm in!" Alia responded.

"Once you complete the pre-work, we can meet, and I can debrief the assignment with you. It'll be great to have you in class. The other participants are really engaged. I think you'll really like them, and I know they'll like you," Whitney assured her sister.

CHAPTER 4
Pre-Work

Alia came back to the office and found the pre-class assignment waiting in her inbox. Before class, Whitney wanted her to log the conversations she has over the next three days including phone calls, face to face interactions, and meetings. Alia used the log without fail over the next few days and made forty-seven entries. Most of the interactions happened spontaneously (one to one meetings in offices, chance meetings in the hallway, or via incoming phone calls), while some others were scheduled in advance. Some of the interactions she had with others were what Alia described as transactional and simple requests, while many others were time consuming, and some were even repeat requests.

While it was not part of the prework assignment, Alia couldn't help but reflect on some of the conversations she had on her list. There were four interactions that stood out as more important to Alia than the others, and that she would like to focus on in some way during class with Whitney. One was a positive interaction, two had less than desirable results, and one was an ongoing unresolved "dilemma" with a senior leader. The positive outcome she enjoyed was with Shayla. Shayla needed Alia's technical expertise to solve an emergent customer problem, which Alia was able to handle while Shayla was talking with the customer, ending in a seamless interaction. Shayla expressed her thanks to Alia, as this could have easily resulted in an upset customer potentially taking their business to a competitor.

On the other side of the ledger, one of the least productive outcomes came when working through an issue yesterday with Cody. Alia became frustrated when Cody did not seem to show a sense of urgency regarding a customer problem that their teams were trying to solve. Cody's lack of engagement seemed to be increasing over the past few weeks, and Alia's team had even approached her about the declining productivity of Cody's team. Alia's team relies on Cody's and vice versa for delivering successful customer outcomes. Alia knew she had to have a "bigger conversation" with him but, had been dreading to approach him about it given their personal friendship.

Unfortunately, Shayla and Alia also had an interaction that took Alia by surprise, and which was less than ideal. More and more lately, Shayla has been asking Alia for immediate answers and data. Shayla's new boss comes from a Big 10 firm and is used to having access to more and different data trends and analytics than NewBuild has ever created. This time, instead of immediately getting to work on what Shayla needed, Alia asked why it was necessary, as the request was not an easy one to achieve. Shayla became clearly frustrated and uncharacteristically cut the interaction short and told Alia to "never mind" and that she would figure something else out and then left the conversation abruptly. While Alia wasn't overly concerned about one less than great interaction with her boss, she certainly didn't want this to become a trend. More than anything though, she was concerned for Shayla as a person, and was anxious to put this past them and get back on track.

The last interaction that occupied some of Alia's thoughts was with the company's General Counsel and member of the senior leadership team, Clint Gaines. Clint is a co-founder of one of the companies that NewBuild acquired over the last year. She does not know Clint well. He recently took over responsibilities for ensuring NewBuild's web compliance matters.

PRE-WORK

Before Clint, Alia worked with an outside firm for compliance needs. While it is early in their relationship, Alia has come to appreciate Clint's legal counsel and quick decision-making. In addition, in their last conversation he also made aesthetic suggestions for the company website that Alia will consider, but she is concerned that Clint seemed to expect these changes to be made.

Alia was looking forward to class and was thankful that it was happening soon.

CHAPTER 5

Debrief

Alia met Whitney at her apartment for dinner later that night. After the sisters enjoyed some time together, they decided to get to the task of reviewing Alia's list. Alia said, "I hope I filled this out right. I'm anxious to know what we're going to do with it now."

"Let's start by looking at who and what is on your list," Whitney suggested. Whitney asked her sister to categorize the entries into three categories: Direct Reports, Colleagues, and her boss. Alia added a fourth category, "C-suite," since she is often visited by members of the senior leadership team directly for technical advice and solutions.

"What common themes do you see from the list, Alia?" Whitney asked.

"Well, I noticed almost as soon as I began keeping track of the interactions, there were many 'repeat customers.' In fact, of the forty-seven entries, most contained repeats of the same people. While that's not surprising on its own, it led me to also note that many of the requests I received were on the same topic and felt very 'reactive.'"

"Were many of the 'repeat customers' on the list with people who you are going to continue to work closely with?" Whitney asked.

"Nearly all of them," Alia replied.

"Last question," Whitney assured her sister.

Alia replied jokingly, "I'll believe that when I hear it."

Now grinning, Whitney asked, "How many of the interactions on the list could have been reduced by you having a proactive conversation with the person at the beginning of the week?"

"I could have seen most of these coming," Alia replied. "No question about that, but Whitney, that's easier said than done."

"I know it is. I really do. I think handling your day-to-day interactions differently is critical to building the type of relationships you want and may even be the leverage you need to bring more joy back to your job," Whitney said with an empathetic tone. "Alia, I want to share some reflections I had regarding what you told me over lunch the other day about missing out on interesting assignments. Are you good with that?" asked Whitney.

Alia assured her she was, and Whitney told her sister that she remembered how interested in technology her sister had been ever since they were little. She went on to joke about how everyone in the family would give Alia any new device that entered their homes to figure out, and then teach back to the "end user," usually one of their parents, how it functioned and how to use it. Then later, their friends would do the same, because Alia never made them feel incompetent for not knowing the technology, and on top of it, was a great teacher. Whitney went on to tell her sister how proud she was of her with her career choice and what she had accomplished thus far. She also told her how she remembered how her sister hated being interrupted when in the middle of well, anything…

They both laughed and Alia admitted, "Nothing much has changed in that regard, especially at work."

Whitney asked her sister, "How do you think your dislike of interruptions has contributed to your current job satisfaction?"

"I've never given it any thought until now," Alia said.

"I want to share something with you called 'the power of contribution' in thinking about interactions." Whitney went on to say, "Sometimes we get so focused on blame and who caused what, that we forget one inescapable fact—if we're part of a situation, we've contributed in some way to its existence and current state. When we focus on our contributions, we may just be able to find a way to improve the whole situation for everyone involved."

Alia was now listening intently to her sister and fought the urge to say, "So, you're saying this is all my fault?" Instead, she thought more about her sister's question and offered, "I am sure I send off signals at times that I don't want to be disturbed, particularly when trying to figure out the best technical solution to a problem."

Whitney then asked, "How do you think others experience your behavior when you're giving off these signals?"

Alia answered, "Unapproachable, I'm sure. And we all hate it when we feel like we're being an imposition on somebody else. I know that."

"So, on your list here, when you approach others and ask for things you need, is that an interruption?" Whitney asked.

"Well, not for me!" Alia replied. "But I get your point. So, what do I do with that?"

"I suggest we start with reframing what you are calling 'interruptions.' In fact, I think your handling of these situations may even be key to earning the types of assignments you have been wanting, because they have to do with building strong, trusting relationships. This starts with being intentional about what you want to accomplish from the conversations you have. In other words, you need to be intentional about desired outcomes before you have the conversation. When you think of it this way, if you have planned for the conversation beforehand, these interactions aren't really interruptions. They are a chance to complete a process you have already begun."

"Thinking about it that way could actually work," Alia said.

"Thanks for the vote of confidence," Whitney replied sarcastically, with a smile. With that, the two called it a night.

CHAPTER 6
Groundwork

Alia arrived at the community college fifteen minutes before class. Whitney, the lead instructor, Brianna, and several participants were already there, so Alia was welcomed and introduced warmly to all. Alia was impressed and somewhat surprised by the age ranges and diverse makeup of the class. Through initial introductions, she met other leaders at local companies, executives of not-for-profit organizations, and students that were just entering the workforce. She felt comfortable with the group already.

The rest of the participants arrived on time. Brianna began class promptly at the beginning of the hour. She reminded the class of their code of conduct which included keeping confidences and listening and speaking with positive intent. One participant spoke up at that point "Is it okay if I share a story about sharing the 'positive intent' ground rule at my organization?" Brianna encouraged her to continue. "At a meeting last week, I shared the concept of 'positive intent' and explained that if we all agree to assume that others are speaking with our best interests and that of the organization, and 'check ourselves' when we speak to make sure we are doing so with positive intent, that we would all benefit greatly. During the meeting, we agreed to try the concept and several times caught ourselves asking if we were speaking and listening with positive intent. We had fun with it, and the quality of the meeting and dialogue were far greater than our usual meetings. We agreed to continue the practice and will be introducing it to the rest of the organization."

After letting the power of the statement sink in, Brianna replied "Well, I cannot think of a better way to begin what we're going to discuss today than with what we just heard." She thanked the participant graciously for her words, let others react, add to the conversation, and then transitioned into formally reintroducing Whitney and thanked her for her willingness to lead class today on the topic of relationship development. With that, she turned the class over to Whitney.

Whitney asked the class to form groups of four to five people. She then said "I'd like to begin today by asking each of you to think about the best conversations in which you've ever engaged. In your groups, I'd like you to discuss what these conversations had in common. Who were they with? What can we learn from them? I'll give you some time to bring these conversations into the room. No need to write anything down. I'll capture our major learnings after you have time to engage in dialogue." With that, the groups set to work on the task Whitney had given them.

Whitney let the groups engage in dialogue for several minutes and then brought the class together again. She stood by a whiteboard and asked participants to name the common characteristics they saw in the examples of great conversations they just had shared.

Characteristics of Great Conversations

- Trust increased after (and during) conversation
- Lots of give and take
- Both parties listened intently (not "waiting to talk")
- Other party was truly curious and interested
- Beginning idea improved as a result of collaboration
- Time seemed to fly by
- Appreciation for the other person's viewpoint grew
- Commitment to the topic being discussed increased
- The conversation kicked off strong & got even stronger
- I felt "heard"
- Conversation flowed

As Whitney wrote, the class engaged in dialogue and noticed that their groups had similar, or the same characteristics. About half-way through the list, one participant offered, "If I could have just one conversation like that during the week, I'd be happy with that."

Whitney added, "We will use this list as our target to shoot for as we plan to have conversations with the characteristics you have so thoughtfully created in this list." After completing the list, Whitney addressed the class and said, "I truly believe that great conversations are the currency of great relationships.

Strengthening relationships, one successful conversation at a time, could be the most strategically important thing leaders can spend their time doing on a day in and day out basis." She continued, "I believe this so strongly in fact that it led me to create a framework called The Conversation Blueprint™ or 'TCB' for planning for and having great conversations."

One participant couldn't help himself and said to Whitney and the class, "TCB – Taking Care of Business."

"I love it!" Whitney replied. After giving the class a second to laugh, she continued. "The characteristics list we just completed represents great outcomes of conversations. Today, we will take the opportunity to examine in detail what goes into making those great conversations well...great. The process we will engage in is much like what baseball players do when they study every aspect of their swing and break down replays from games to identify specific ways to improve their mechanics before their games, or when a ballerina meticulously practices her craft, one position at a time so that she can leap into flight at the exact right time. What I'm going to show you now is a template you can use to plan for important conversations. The template mirrors the process I take my clients through as they prepare to have great conversations." With that, she displayed the template.

Groundwork	Conversation Plan
Name:	Next Step:
Position:	Approach:
Situation:	Positional Impact:
Objective:	Pace:
Trust Level:	Success Description:
Comm. Driver:	Opening:
Considerations:	

Whitney continued, "As you can see, the tool is divided into two sections - Groundwork and Conversation Plan. The Groundwork section contains multiple choice and free answer sections, designed to help you analyze the situation in which you are about to engage. The Conversation Plan has some sections whose 'answers' are driven by responses previously given as part of Groundwork."

With that, Whitney began explaining the tool, beginning with identifying the Position of the coworker with whom you will be having the conversation. She then said, "The slides I'm going to share with you now represent the possible selections for each category of The Conversation Blueprint that you can use for note taking purposes as we discuss them.

Position

- ❑ Direct Report
- ❑ Colleague
- ❑ My Direct Manager
- ❑ C-Suite/Sr. Leader

Notes:

The position of the coworker with whom you will be talking has an impact on both what you plan to accomplish and how you get there. We will cover this thoroughly when we discuss the "Position Impact" category of the conversation plan. For now, it is helpful to have in mind the hierarchical relationship we share with our coworkers as we frame the rest of the conversation."

She then segued to the next topic. "Situation Summary is an open answer space for you to provide the main elements of the reason behind having the conversation. After thinking about the conversation, and for many of us, important conversations can roll around in our brains for a long time (too long). It is an excellent idea to boil the issue down to its key elements. For this reason, the situation summary should be no more than thirty words.

Situation Summary

Briefly (30 words or less) describe the situation (the problem to be solved, critical context, decision to be made, etc.) you will be framing.

The Situation Summary should cover the problem to be solved, decision to be made, and any critical context that could impact the ensuing conversation with your coworker." Whitney noticed that participants were taking notes and looking up as if they were trying to summarize their own upcoming situations. Whitney said, "Why don't you each pick an upcoming situation you will be having. Now with the person next to you, share your situations and then summarize it with the help of your partner."

The class split into pairs and were commenting on how hard it can be to summarize their situations. Whitney asked if anyone was willing to share an example. Alia's partner encouraged Alia to share hers. Alia obliged by sharing the upcoming conversation she planned to have with Shayla. "Recent change in boss's approach and stress level since getting a new boss are concerning. We had a rough recent conversation that I don't want to impact the relationship." The class and Whitney agreed that her example was a good one, prompting others to share their summaries.

Alia couldn't help but think to herself how helpful it was to spend time thinking about upcoming conversations before having them. While this is not her normal practice, she was beginning to understand the value of it. As if reading her mind, Whitney addressed the class. "Thinking through what you want to accomplish is so important. We will continue to devote time to this topic, including the situation summary, and the next section as well, Conversation Objective.

Conversation Objective

- ❏ Make decision
- ❏ Deliver feedback or input
- ❏ Ask for something (resources, help, budget, etc.)
- ❏ Apologize
- ❏ Listen deeply to understand & show support for coworker
- ❏ Gather data or input
- ❏ Communicate information (decision made, project update, etc.)
- ❏ Provide direction/set expectations (usually reserved for direct reports)
- ❏ Solve business problem
- ❏ De-escalate or defuse situation (misunderstanding, interpersonal conflict, etc.)
- ❏ Clarify boundaries or rules of engagement
- ❏ Change in behavior
- ❏ Improve performance in a particular area
- ❏ Other_____

Take the same conversation you just summarized. Now, see if you can identify the overall objective using the list above. Anybody willing to share?"

With that, one participant shared that her goal for an upcoming conversation with a colleague was clearly to land on a decision. Other participants identified different objectives. Alia also participated in the dialogue and shared that she was thinking of several upcoming conversations, each with a different objective.

After the rich discussion, Whitney asked if participants had questions about the value of identifying the overall objective of a key conversation. One participant shared that he saw the value and was hoping that the class would spend some time discussing problem solving conversations as he saw the difference between this type of conversation and others. Immediately, other participants identified other types of conversations they saw as critical.

Whitney addressed the class and said, "While each type of conversation is different and has its nuances and associated best practices that you can integrate into your planning for the conversation, we will focus our time and energy in this class on the factors that impact success and that apply to all types of conversations. This includes the level of trust you have with the other person, their communication style, and your specific definition of success." Whitney then continued to the next category.

"I'm sure it is no surprise to see this next category of analysis—Trust Level—in the other person with whom you'll be speaking. Assessing our level of trust with those we're having conversations with is the most critical element in determining our overall approach to the conversation. It is also a goal to having great conversations—increasing trusting relationships.

Trust Level with Coworker

- ❑ Inner Circle
- ❑ Strong
- ❑ Developing
- ❑ Neutral
- ❑ Cautious
- ❑ Low/Weak
- ❑ Untested/New

Notes:

Assessing the level of trust is based on the success of past conversations and the degree that the relationship has been 'tested' or not. By tested, I am referring to whether you have worked with the other person in the past to solve problems, make decisions, etc. and have been able to form an opinion as to whether you feel that person acts consistently and with integrity.

The choice of 'Inner Circle' is reserved for those with whom you trust implicitly and have no reservation in saying whatever you feel needs to be said. These are the 'go to' individuals you approach when you want the unvarnished truth and who you know have your best interests at heart. Those with whom you have a 'Strong' level of trust are the next candidates in line to become part of your inner circle. These are people you have had excellent interactions with in the past, with the only thing left to prove is consistency over more time. Trust that is 'Developing' describes newer coworker relationships that are going well, 'so far so good,' but have not yet really been tested. 'Neutral' trust describes those coworkers with whom you only occasionally work and/or have not made your mind up about yet. A good strategy for those falling into this category is to schedule a 'meeting before the meeting' when you know you'll be working with them to share your views and better understand theirs proactively. The learning you get from doing this helps to tee up the larger conversation for success.

We all have coworkers with whom we either don't often agree, or for one reason or another exercise 'Caution' when dealing with them. I've heard colleagues describe people fitting into this category as those with whom they have seen 'yellow flags' (situations where we "suspect" the person didn't act with our best interests in mind) in terms of whether we feel we find them trustworthy. There are hopefully very few coworkers we work with who fall into "Low/Weak" category of trust. These are people with whom we feel we see 'red flags' (situations or patterns we've seen from several situations where we witness or believe the person is not acting in our best interests) when dealing with them, and/or have a difficult time trusting them based on past experiences.

Lastly, those we don't know or have not yet had our relationships tested, fall into the "Untested/New" category. Working with people for the first time represents great opportunities for successful relationship builders. Perhaps the new person brings with them critical skills, or networks, or is simply a colleague that values collaboration."

At this point, Whitney gave the group a twenty-minute break that included the task of choosing a few coworkers with whom they expect to soon have conversations and applying their level of trust with these individuals using a "trust grid." Alia's completed trust grid is shown below.

	C-Suite	Direct Mgr.	Colleagues	Dir. Reports
Inner Circle			Cody W.	
Strong		Shayla M.		Darius R.
Developing	Clint G.			
Neutral				
Cautious				
Low/Weak				
Untested/New				

After the break, Whitney asked participants to share their completed grids with each other and discuss their reactions to the exercise. Many expressed a desire to have more people in their inner circle, others were concerned that they did not enjoy strong trust with any of their coworkers, and some felt they trusted everyone as strong or above and weren't sure this was "real" upon reflection. All agreed that trust was a key consideration in having great conversations and that they wanted to have as many trusting relationships as they could develop.

This subject piqued a great deal of interest in the class. One participant offered, "My inner circle is more the size of a golf ball than a basketball." Others laughed, and the class started to engage in a great conversation around the topic. With that, Whitney invited the group to further discuss what they thought of their inner circle, if it needed more or fewer people, and if they are getting what they need from them. The class agreed that they wanted their inner circles to include at least a few more people. The dialogue also culminated in identifying and discussing the shared traits of those in our inner circle.

- Credibility across organization
- Keeps confidences
- Tell us what we need to hear
- Listens deeply
- Treats me, self, and others with respect
- Consistently adds value & insight

After thanking the group for their engagement, Whitney continued by saying, "Let's continue with the next category, Communication Driver.

Coworker's Communication Driver

❑ Results
❑ Relationships
❑ Precision
❑ Harmony
Notes:

Each of us has a unique personality and preference for communicating and receiving information. For our purposes, we will want to know the most successful way to present information to the other person. I have found four major communication drivers that most motivate the other person with whom I am speaking:

- Results — Those interested in results want us to get to the point quickly without a lot of small talk. These are the people that want us to <u>bottom-line</u> our messages, what we want from them, etc. They prefer to focus on the problem at hand, or decision to be made, rather than take extra time for relationship-building.

- Relationships — Relationship-driven people are usually outgoing and gregarious and want to connect personally during the conversation, as well as get to business. They are <u>people-people</u> and will often ask how you are doing and show genuine interest in you as well as the topic at hand. Relationship-driven people don't tend to resist change too strongly as long as they see the benefit that they and others will gain as a result. In fact, they may well be great supporters of change initiatives, particularly if they see personal benefit in it.

- Precision — Those interested in precision want data and facts to lead the way. They prefer taking their time to come to the <u>right answer.</u> They can be described as perfectionists and could frustrate others by their perceived aversion to change, and not moving quickly enough for some. They are driven by <u>doing it right the first time.</u> For those who are driven by precision, we will want to make sure we have our facts straight before talking with them, and likely will want to share pertinent information with them before engaging in conversation.

- Harmony — Those driven by harmony are most interested in everyone getting along and being happy. They prefer to not engage in 'changing just for the sake of changing.' They want to ensure that decisions are thoroughly thought through and that what is being newly proposed won't negatively impact or replace what they view as currently working well, or at least well enough.

Knowing your coworker's predominant communication style is critical in planning for a successful outcome, and among other things, helps with deciding the right pace for the conversation. We don't often naturally think about adjusting our style to meet the needs of others, and this is a critical characteristic of both the best listeners and of great conversations.

Of course, all people are unique and never fit neatly into any one box or style. Still, it is helpful to observe what is driving someone's behavior and then flex our style to achieve outcomes that will satisfy all parties."

Whitney and the group then began laughing at one participant's attempt to adapt to Whitney's facilitation style. After the levity died down a bit, Whitney continued. "That's a great segue to our next activity! I'd like you now to identify what you think is your communication driver. Once you have what you think your driver is, turn to the person next to you, share what your communication driver is, and why you believe this to be the case."

The class members then each freely shared their own communication driver. Some said one of the four was clearly their predominant driver, while others said they thought they had a blended style. "We want to know what our style is, particularly so we can keep ourselves 'in check' with the other person's style. I know my driver is Relationships, and as such can sometimes not cover the information those valuing Results and Precision may need." Whitney said. Alia was confident that "results" is her communication driver. She wondered in what ways this helped and hindered her conversations and relationships with others. She believed that Shayla shared her style, while Cody's communication driver was harmony. She thought Clint was most likely focused on precision. Given how different each of these people are, it made sense to her to vary her communication style, although she wasn't quite sure yet how to do that.

Whitney continued, "Finally, to ensure that all the specific factors of the situation you'll be discussing are included in setting up your conversation for success, the next section includes an open answer question designed to elicit any other factors to consider that could impact the success of the conversation."

Other Considerations

Are there any other considerations (friends outside of work, fear that having the conversation may make the situation worse, new executive – my boss' boss just hired, etc.) that could materially impact the successful outcome of the conversation?

"There are myriad issues occurring and decisions being made in any organization at any time. This space asks you to consider those that may materially impact the conversation, or that you feel are important. Sometimes, we find ourselves in situations where we need to have performance conversations with close friends. Through an organizational restructuring effort, I once was given the assignment to manage someone whose wedding I was in the next month. Pretending these things don't at least enter our thought process is disingenuous. This section is meant to elicit these things, allow us to name them, and critically evaluate how relevant (or irrelevant) they are to the success of the conversation we are going to have. The steps you've just completed should now give you a good idea of how to set the groundwork for a successful, important conversation. These steps may even be as important as breaking for lunch is!" Whitney smiled as she told the class they would reconvene in an hour.

During the lunch hour, Alia thought about what Whitney said about relationships being built one conversation at a time. She was hopeful that implementing the practices of TCB would allow her to build relationships more effectively with the upcoming conversations she had. Maybe she would even eventually see the value of impromptu drop-ins as value added activities instead of interruptions? Thinking that made her laugh as she finished her lunch.

CHAPTER 7
Conversation Plan

Groundwork	Conversation Plan
Name:	Next Step:
Position:	Approach:
Situation:	Positional Impact:
Objective:	Pace:
Trust Level:	Success Description:
Comm. Driver:	Opening:
Considerations:	

Whitney and the class came back from lunch on time and were discussing the subject matter they'd covered in the morning. Whitney addressed the group and asked if they were ready to get started with part two of The Conversation Blueprint process, creating the Conversation Plan.

Next Step

- ☐ Schedule 1-1 meeting
- ☐ Wait until right time arises organically
- ☐ Do not have conversation at present
- ☐ Discuss during next regularly scheduled meeting
- ☐ Other

Notes:

The group nodded with all the post lunch vigor they could muster. Whitney began by saying "The Next Step involves your considering whether you'll be engaging in conversation with your coworker and how you plan to ensure it happens."

A participant in class asked, "Is there ever a time when you don't want to go through with a conversation?"

"In my experience, absolutely! There have been plenty of times when after fleshing out a situation, we discover it involves more people than we think, more potential negative consequences, etc. In those cases, the decision is often made to get more information before talking with the other person, or the best decision sometimes really is to not engage."

After a short back and forth dialogue in class where participants gave some examples of when not to have conversations, Whitney continued. "The next three categories are decided by responses completed during Groundwork. You can always change or add context to the suggested response if you see fit. We will start with the Overall Approach to the conversation," Whitney told the class.

Overall Approach

- ☐ Guarded and Open
- ☐ Cautious Optimism
- ☐ Set the Stage for a Great Relationship
- ☐ Go First with Vulnerability
- ☐ Full Openness

Notes:

Whitney continued and said, "In TCB, the overall approach is determined by the level of trust you enjoy, or don't yet enjoy, with the other party. Each approach is based on improving the current level of trust with the other party, while reflecting on your current relationship with them. With those where trust has been weak in the past, a Guarded and Open approach is suggested where you focus on the task at hand without going into the past or down 'side roads' during the conversation. While great relationships are built one great conversation at a time, poor relationships can also be improved one conversation at a time. With those whom we feel we need to be cautious (we've seen 'yellow flags'), Cautious Optimism is the preferred approach. This approach suggests staying on track with the current conversation and looking for ways to improve the relationship by finding common ground with our coworker during the conversation. Since this relationship has had at least some 'ups,' there is reason to think there may be something on which to build. If the conversation at hand goes well and presents an opportunity to discover common interests and other opportunities for collaboration, take advantage of it. With new coworkers and those with whom you haven't worked, the Set the Stage for a Great Relationship approach works best. You certainly know how to do that!" With that, Whitney referenced the chart listing characteristics of great conversations, which they had completed earlier in class.

Characteristics of Great Conversations

- Trust increased after (and during) conversation
- **Lots of give and take**
- Both parties listened intently (not "waiting to talk")
- **Other party was truly curious and interested**
- Beginning idea improved as a result of collaboration
- **Time seemed to fly by**
- Appreciation for the other person's viewpoint grew
- **Commitment to the topic being discussed increased**
- The conversation kicked off strong & got even stronger
- **I felt "heard"**
- Conversation flowed

Whitney continued, "For those with whom we enjoy neutral, strong, or developing trust, the conversation at hand presents a wonderful opportunity to further solidify the relationship and perhaps add to your 'inner circle.' The thought you've put into the upcoming conversation should only add to what has been a very productive relationship. Going First with Vulnerability means that you can say what needs to be said—always with tact—by sharing how you view the situation and deeply listening to the other party. Given your respect for the other person, if their views differ from yours, you'll be presented with a great opportunity to expand your knowledge of the current situation without fear of the other party's intentions. You may even decide to pivot on your original stance based on what you learn. With those in your 'inner circle,' you can exercise Full Openness. Those in your inner circle represent a great opportunity for you to test your understanding of situations and show vulnerability. You can ask for advice, ways to improve, and test whether you have any blind spots around the topic at hand. Those in your inner circle operate with positive intent and are also willing to tell you what you need to hear, even if you may not want to hear it."

Alia was happy that she enjoys several close relationships where she could take advantage of being fully open. She also saw the difference in how she had to prepare and think with those she did not enjoy trusting relationships. She thought to herself how much more time it takes to get productive outcomes with those we don't enjoy strong trust. Time that she did not have.

The class again discussed the importance of being able to enjoy work relationships where full openness was the norm. After thanking the class for the rich dialogue, Whitney segued to the next topic by saying, "We are now going to discuss another consideration in having great conversations and that is derived from your hierarchical relationship with the other person. Positional Impact.

Considering the hierarchical relationship of your coworker matters, particularly when it comes to deciding the appropriate amount of influence (as opposed to direct authority or 'decision rights') you can employ during the conversation. While it's perfectly reasonable to provide clear direction and performance expectations to your direct reports, leading through 'influence' is critical when dealing with your boss or a member of the C-suite. Leading through influence means having an impact on the behaviors, decisions, and choices of others through authentically sharing your views and their potential benefits, without manipulating or directing the other person to do things your way. The major impact of your coworker's position is summarized as follows.

Positional Impact

- ❏ Direct Reports = You have decision rights
- ❏ Colleague = Neutral
- ❏ Direct Manager = They have decision rights
- ❏ C-Suite = Heavy time & responsibility demands

Notes:

When talking with your Direct Manager, it is important to know that no matter the situation and how strong the relationship, the direct leader has the final say, or "decision rights." This is a key difference between having conversations with your direct leader and other constituents. We may not agree with the decision, however it is important to remember that the leader is within their purview to make that decision, which helps us maintain positive intent and decorum throughout the conversation. Additionally, waiting to 'be asked in' is the preferred method of providing behavioral feedback to your direct leader. Obviously with 'bad news' about the business, it is always preferable to not let your direct leader be surprised. With behavioral feedback or advice, if possible, being invited to share your thoughts first is a safe way of knowing that your words have the best chance of being well received.

With Senior Leaders/C-Suite, maintaining respect and acknowledging we do not know the whole story is always important. This is particularly true with senior leaders, as their time and responsibility demands are extremely heavy. We don't know what decisions and issues senior leaders, and often our direct managers, are dealing with. Particularly in the case of our direct manager, we may not know, nor may we ever know, the ways they may be helping, or even protecting us in conversations.

With Colleagues, the positional impact is neutral, in that there are usually no real hierarchical considerations. This is one advantage of having colleagues in your inner circle, as they can provide balanced feedback without political pressure or competing considerations.

In working with your Direct Reports, you have decision rights and the ability to set direction unilaterally. Developing direct reports through listening, dialogue, and coaching are more powerful and effective tools, particularly in the long run. Remembering the characteristics of great conversations is every bit as important when you have positional power as when you don't."

Alia pictured herself having conversations with Cody, Shayla, Clint, and her direct reports. For the first time, she thought about the impact of a person's position relative to one's own on a conversation's success. A pattern of different strategies for upcoming conversations was emerging for her.

CONVERSATION PLAN

Whitney then asked the group to go back for a moment to talk about the relationship makeup (Colleagues? Boss? Direct Reports? C-suite?) of their "inner circles." The vast majority of those in the inner circle are constituted of colleagues at a similar level. "Why do you think that is?" Whitney asked. After some discussion, the group landed on a few reasons for this—colleagues are at a similar level and share similar issues, having direct reports in our inner circle can create hard feelings among other team members, and even damage productivity, and lastly, that it's always "a bit of a dance" when talking with your boss, because as collaborative as they may be, the element of hierarchy is always present in the background.

Whitney perceived that the group was getting excited and ready to apply the tool to their own situations now. Sensing this, Whitney continued, "Listening to the conversations now and hearing the ways you can apply the concepts of The Conversation Blueprint is gratifying and we're now going to look at the suggested 'pace' for the conversation, based on the other party's communication driver. Remember that our goal is to have consistently <u>great</u> conversations. To achieve the same level of excellent results among different stakeholders, we need to use decidedly different approaches.

Pace

- ❑ Get to the "bottom line" quickly
- ❑ Greet personally, move quickly & collaboratively
- ❑ Focus on the facts, then move deliberately
- ❑ Focus on the people impact & move deliberately

Notes:

The Pace section of the tool coincides with the response given to the Communication Driver you selected in the Groundwork section as follows:

- Results = Get to the 'bottom line' quickly

- Relationships = Greet personally, move quickly and collaboratively

- Precision = Focus on the facts, then move deliberately

- Harmony = Focus on the people impact and move deliberately

While we've already identified our communication drivers and preferences, tailoring the pace of the conversation to meet the needs of the other party allows them to hear our messages more effectively. This increases the chances of having a great conversation.

Getting to the bottom line quickly involves providing the reason for the meeting and what you need from the other party up front. Knowing the purpose and what is needed allows those whose focus is Results to dive into what they see as 'the meat' of the conversation without focusing on 'unnecessary' delays or pleasantries. This doesn't mean you shouldn't greet your coworker. It simply means that once doing so, get to the subject at hand.

Greet personally, move quickly and collaboratively is the preferred approach for those who most value Relationships. Many executives who are described as having 'great communication' or 'people' skills fall into this category. Greet them warmly and if you get the feeling that the other person wants to chat or get to know you more after you initially greet one another, before moving directly into the business need at hand, go with it! Once the business need begins, be ready for them to want to play an active role in coming to the decision and to keep the conversation flowing freely and quickly, hence the 'collaboratively' part of the equation. You may need to gently reel them in to keep them focused and meet time requirements."

One participant added, "I know that person!" Another added, "I am that person!"

After the levity subsided, Whitney spoke again. "Moving on…Conversely, other coworkers prefer focusing on making sure that they have all the facts needed, particularly when making decisions and solving problems. This is where the strategy of Focusing on the Facts and then Moving Deliberately makes sense. People who desire precision prefer to move deliberately (or slowly at times) to ensure there are no 'i's left undotted or t's left uncrossed.' You may have to guard against the possibility of 'analysis paralysis' with coworkers who share this communication style. Reminding them gently of the goal and time constraints is necessary on these occasions. Those who desire harmony want to ensure that conversations Focus on People Impact and Move Deliberately, as opposed to 'changing things just for the sake of making changes.' It is important to let these coworkers know the impact any changes or decisions will have on people as a result of the decisions we make. To the degree possible, it is important during conversations to highlight the ways we have thought through any changes we suggest and the rationale or 'why' behind them."

Whitney then addressed the class by saying, "The next slide asks you to define what success 'looks like' before having the conversation. To do this, you will need to respond to the following prompt."

Success Description

Imagine you had the conversation with your coworker and that it went great! How would you know? (agreements, decisions or topics raised, tone of the conversation, feeling afterward, etc.)

Whitney asked, "Any volunteers willing to take a shot at how you'd describe success for any of your upcoming conversations?" After a few moments, several participants shared their thoughts.

"We would agree on a decision and stick with it."

"My coworker would say they felt deeply listened to."

"I would learn, specifically what my boss expects."

"We'd have a shared sense of a go-forward direction."

"My colleague would <u>hear</u> my apology."

At this point, Alia spoke and said, "It sounds like such an obvious practice to adopt, but I really don't think through what success would look and feel like before I go into meetings and even important conversations." At that point, other participants agreed and nodded their heads.

Whitney added, "You're clearly not alone, Alia. If there is one thing you can do differently upon leaving this class to improve conversations immediately, it is to think through successful outcomes in advance."

Addressing the whole class, Whitney said, "Finally, once you have analyzed the important elements that will make this conversation a great one, it is advisable to script out your opening sentence or two. Just as professional football teams script their first few plays in advance of the game to 'set the tone' of how they want to play the game, you want to do the same thing to ensure you begin the conversation well."

> **Opening**
>
> "I want to talk about our last conversation when you were looking for the search data on our consulting services. I didn't feel like you got what you needed from me."

After thanking both Whitney and Alia, Brianna stood up at this point and moved to the front of the room. She announced that the homework for the next class would be to frame several (4 - 6) upcoming conversations using TCB. This prompted one participant to ask, "Hey, does Alia get out of doing this?!?!?!" Through laughter, Whitney replied, "Oh no! She gets to work with me one-on-one on her assignment."

CHAPTER 8
Post-Work

Alia left class both hopeful and unsure about the amount of time conversation framing would take on top of her already packed workload. While she didn't want to hurt her sister's feelings, she decided to raise her concerns gently when she next spoke with Whitney.

Later that week, Alia met Whitney after work. As was their custom, they worked through dinner while also catching up. Whitney applauded her sister for choosing a variety of different stakeholders with whom to frame upcoming conversations during class. Alia was about to share how she prepared to approach her upcoming conversation with Cody, when she felt a sense of uneasiness. Just then she blurted out, "Whit, I appreciate so much all that you've done for me. The class and the tools are phenomenal. I don't know if I can fill out a template like this for every interaction I have and do everything else expected of me." Well played. So much for bringing this up "gently," Alia thought to herself sarcastically.

Whitney waited a minute for her sister to be in the right place to hear the next part of their conversation, and then continued. "I believe that if you become more deliberate about the conversations you are about to have with just the people you identified in the assignment, this will go a long way toward improving the quality of your interactions, and in building the type of deep relationships necessary to succeed as an executive."

When Whitney said the word executive, Alia immediately had a reaction. She told her sister that the other area of improvement she received on her 360 review was to develop her executive presence and ability to think strategically. Alia admitted to her sister that while she didn't know exactly what 'executive presence' means, she did know the advice had to do with improving her people skills.

Whitney said, "Many of my clients also struggle with thinking and acting strategically when they are constantly called upon to fix and deal with what's happening in the here and now. If you want to have more conversations about developing your strategic thinking muscles specifically, I'm all in. Of course, strategic thinking and executive presence are closely related. As far as executive presence goes, every outstanding executive I know has a GREAT network built on a solid foundation of strong relationships cultivated over a career of hard work."

Alia took a minute to let what her sister said sink in and remembered her words from class. Building and strengthening relationships now, one successful conversation at a time, could be the most strategically important thing she could spend her time doing. She began to feel the anxiety replaced by cautious hopefulness. Alia knew that what her sister said made sense. The sisters then decided to focus on the discussion Alia would be having soon with her close friend and colleague, Cody Wilkes.

CHAPTER 9
TCB with Colleagues

Whitney said, "Alia, before you show me your conversation frame for Cody, why don't we just talk about the situation." Whitney knew Cody through Alia and liked him very much. She was certainly appreciative that he had helped Alia land her current job. "Is the issue with Cody a new one?" Whitney asked.

Alia replied, "Cody's been having difficulty with a couple of his team members, and it has been getting worse over the last few weeks. He doesn't have a handle on how to deal with it. Meanwhile, of course, it is impacting my team's productivity, because much of the work we do is intertwined; our teams are on the same projects and share resources and clients as well."

"Has Cody spoken with his boss about the situation?" Whitney asked.

"He has, but his boss is so taken up with acquisitions that he has no time for him, so Cody's been coming to me for help, and that puts me in a weird place," Alia said.

Whitney was curious about her sister's last response, so she asked, "Why is that weird for you? Is it because he's a friend outside of work?"

"Yeah. That, and when his team struggles, my team complains to me, and I feel I need to have their backs."

"I see. You're right, of course, about all of that. We can't ignore elements of our relationships when we are striving to have great conversations that positively impact performance. And I don't think we should. Cody being a friend presents both a challenge and an opportunity. Cody is someone you care deeply about. I'd guess that you are in his inner circle. There's no reason to not let that come through when you talk with him next. It sounds like he needs a friend as much as anything else right now," Whitney said.

Alia let out a sigh of relief at this point and said, "I think I needed to hear that, or at least have permission to let our friendship matter at work. It's tricky stuff when you blend worlds. Way more complicated than I thought," Alia said.

"It is for sure," her sister countered, "I'll bet in ways it's wonderful. At least it can be."

"It may be for this reason that I had such a hard time landing on a success description."

"Crafting desired outcomes really is a surprisingly hard thing to do, and not just for conversations—for anything. It's hard work. Most leaders are so used to reacting to the issues of the day that getting ahead of something can feel foreign," Whitney assured her sister. "In fact, I learned this the hard way with one of my very first clients," Whitney continued. "I remember being really excited for this project and preparing for my first meeting with the executive sponsoring it. I decided to begin by asking him what his vision was for the project I was working on. He had some ideas but needed help thinking through how to clearly describe what he wanted. It was clear that during the conversation he was a bit embarrassed and trying to find his words on the fly, because he really didn't know yet what he wanted. And he's not alone in this! I've now come to expect this and plan to help craft desired outcomes as part of the regular process I facilitate with clients. Most people need to 'iterate' a bit before they come to what they really want."

"That makes more sense to me, than you can possibly know." With that, Alia said goodnight to her sister and headed home.

The next morning, Alia reviewed her conversation plan for Cody and felt more prepared than she ever had been for a conversation in her life.

Groundwork	Conversation Plan
Name: Cody Wilkes	**Next Step:** Schedule 1-1 meeting
Position: Colleague	**Approach:** Full openness
Situation: Cody's struggling in his role which is frustrating my team, who work closely with his.	**Positional Impact:** Neutral
	Pace: Move deliberately & focus on people impact
Objective: Listen deeply to understand & show support for coworker	**Success Description:** Cody leaves conversation feeling heard and with a next steps plan.
Trust Level: Inner Circle	
Comm. Driver: Harmony	
Considerations: Close friend outside of work.	**Opening:** Thanks for making the time to talk. I wanted to finish the conversation we had in my office last week. I was pressed for time and didn't feel like I listened well.

After a meeting that she and Cody were participating in concluded, they went across the hall to Cody's office as planned. Alia then began the conversation with Cody. "Thanks for making the time to talk. I wanted to finish the conversation we had in my office last week. I was pressed for time and didn't feel like I listened too well."

"Wow. Thanks. That's a relief," Cody said.

"Why is it a relief, Cody?"

"It's just that it seems that every work-related conversation that anyone wants to have with me lately has to do with some aspect of my team that's not going well," Cody explained.

"Then, I'm even more glad we can spend some time on what matters to you," Alia assured her friend. "What's going on?"

Cody went on to explain several issues that he'd been having. Alia reminded herself frequently, "Cody's communication driver is 'Harmony' and he's a trusted friend—don't interrupt!" She heeded her own advice well as Cody said, "So, now that you've let me go on and on about all of my issues, do you have any advice?"

"First, how about we narrow down the issue for which you most need help," Alia said with a tone that let Cody know she was joking. The two friends shared a laugh and then Cody continued.

"Yeah. That's a good idea. Firstly, I want your honest opinion. Has any of what I've told you about what I'm experiencing, or feeling been a shock to you?"

"No, I'm not shocked. Since you have now described in more detail how things have been, and more importantly how you are personally impacted, I definitely have a better grasp of the full context."

"Look, Alia, I know that my team's and my struggle impacts you and your team, and I feel terrible about it. I'm not sure where to go next and could use your take on the situation, advice, and help."

"Okay, Cody. Do I have your permission to be one hundred percent honest?" Alia asked her friend.

"Thanks for letting me brace for impact first, and yeah, shoot," Cody replied.

"Recently, Whitney shared with me how she thinks each person is motivated by one of four dominant communication drivers." Alia then briefly explained the four drivers and asked, "Which one do you think is yours?"

"Do I even need to say it? It's clearly Harmony."

"I agree. It is one of the things I admire most about you. You're an incredible listener. All our friends go to you first with important issues and problems. It's normally a wonderful strength, as you not only want everyone to get along, but you also make sure we do, even when that's not easy. At work, given the current white water change our company is experiencing, I wonder if perhaps your drive for harmony is blocking the need for real change to occur within your team right now," Alia replied.

Cody slumped in his chair and breathed out a huge breath. "Yeah. I think you hit on something big here. I'll probably need more time to process the full implications of this, but ever since the Axis acquisition when we added their suite of consulting services, I've felt like I've been playing catch up. When we acquired Teltex three months later, that added another differentiated service and bolstered Axis' suite. That's when all the stuff I just downloaded on you began. I've been overwhelmed, or at least 'whelmed,' ever since and I'm still there," Cody said.

"I've had to change a couple of processes since those acquisitions as well. I realize now, through our conversation, that you could have benefited from knowing earlier what I learned about them. In the future, I'll make sure you're more in the loop. For now, if it would help, I can let you know what I did to accommodate the new company services. It seems to be working well." Alia saw her friend appear more relieved as she finished speaking.

"Thanks, Alia. I'll take you up on your offer. Can we talk again later this week? I have a lot to think about and I feel so much better after talking to you and can at least start to see a bit of light at the end of the tunnel. Much appreciated, my friend," Cody said.

"I'm just glad to see you looking and talking a bit more hopefully, Cody." Cody nodded in agreement and the two ended their meeting.

CHAPTER 10

TCB with Your Direct Leader

Alia was so encouraged by her conversation with Cody that she decided to complete the TCB template for her upcoming conversation with Shayla before going home that evening. Alia recalled Whitney's key tips in planning conversations with one's direct leader.

1. Remember that no matter the situation and how strong the relationship, the direct leader has the final say, or "decision rights." This is a key difference between having conversations with your direct leader and other constituents. We may not agree with the decision, however remembering that the leader is within her purview to make it can help us maintain positive intent and decorum throughout the conversation.

2. Maintaining respect and acknowledging that we do not know the whole story is always important, and particularly so with your direct leader and senior leaders. We do not know what our leader is being called to do, or in what ways they may be helping (or even protecting) us in conversations to which we are not, and may never be, privy.

3. Waiting to "be asked in" is the preferred method of providing behavioral feedback to your direct leader. Obviously with "bad news" about the

business, it is always preferable to not let your direct leader be surprised. With behavioral feedback or advice, if possible, being invited to share your thoughts first is a safe way of knowing that your words have the best chance of being well received.

Alia decided to think about and write down (writing things down is a process Alia has come to rely on in helping her sort through and better remember important issues) key elements of her upcoming conversation with Shayla.

- Shayla has recently begun asking me for more and different information than she has in the past, and her need to have the information quickly has also become more urgent.

- Shayla and I get along extremely well and enjoy a very supportive and professional relationship. I have learned a great deal from her and admire her as a leader. We have weathered storms together and while we disagree at times, the disagreements only seem to make our relationship stronger.

- Shayla and I share the same communication driver, but it looks different on us. Shayla is usually (though not lately) more patient than I am, although she is all about making decisions and moving forward.

- She has a new boss. One thing that I learned from spending some time in quality assurance is that when there are sudden changes including drops in performance, broken processes, and behavioral changes, the first place to look in finding out "why" is to discover what has recently changed in the system. In this case, it is clearly the change in Shalya's boss, and by association my "big boss" as well.

- Shayla has been an excellent mentor while allowing me to "drive" when decisions fall more into my areas of expertise than hers. I really want to make sure we don't lose what we have.

- I want to get on the table what Shayla needs from me and to give her the opportunity to share and discuss openly what has changed for her with Mitch's hiring if she feels inclined to do so. I will make space for her without pushing the envelope.

With that, Alia completed the template and went home for the evening.

Groundwork	Conversation Plan
Name: Shayla Maye **Position:** Direct Manager **Situation:** Recent change in boss' approach and stress level since getting a new boss are concerning. We had rough recent conversation that I don't want to impact relationship. **Objective:** De-escalate or Defuse Situation **Trust Level:** High **Comm. Driver:** Results **Considerations:** Shayla has a new boss and pressures.	**Next Step:** Discuss during next regularly scheduled meeting **Approach**: Go first, be vulnerable **Positional Impact:** Boss has decision rights **Pace:** Get to the point of the conversation/bottom line quickly **Success Description:** Get on the table what Shayla needs from me and give her opportunity to share and discuss what has changed. **Opening:** I want to talk about our last conversation when you were looking for data on our consulting services. I didn't feel like you got what you needed from me.

The next morning at 10:00 a.m. Alia was in her office, about to take advantage of an hour she had free before her next meeting, when Shayla showed up at her door.

"Do you have time to talk?" Shayla asked.

"Absolutely," Alia said as she offered her manager a chair.

"I just wanted to apologize for being so short with you last week, Alia. I feel awful and I'm sorry it took me this long to tell you so," Shayla offered.

Alia thought to herself, (Well, I'm glad I planned for this conversation yesterday instead of later in the week, when I originally planned to.) She then recalled the crux of her success description.

> "Get on the table what Shayla needs from me and give her
> the opportunity to share what's changed for her."

"Thanks for that. There are no apologies necessary, Shayla. I didn't take it personally, and I'm glad you brought it up. I've been wondering if I'm giving you the right amount of information and if perhaps your needs in this area have changed," Alia said.

"Well, my needs haven't changed," Shayla said, "But my new boss wants a lot more than my former one, that's for sure."

"I wondered if that might be the case," Alia admitted.

"Don't get me wrong, Mitch is extremely smart and has a ton of knowledge that we, and I, can benefit from, but we are both so busy that he often asks for things that aren't always easy to get and often doesn't talk about why he needs them. Then of course, I will pass that on to you. It's not fair to you and I know it needs to change, Alia."

"It seems that a lot of the data he's looking for is for benchmarking purposes, is that right?"

"You are spot on. He is compiling a ninety-day observations and strategy implications deck for the CEO and of course, you don't know what you're going to discover when you're doing a business analysis until you get into it," Shayla said.

"I think I could be of help here. I won't know for sure until I know exactly what he wants. Do you remember the stuff I had to compile for Project Copernicus last year that ended in our passing on an acquisition of that start-up data mining firm?" Alia asked her boss.

"I forgot all about that! I can't keep up with companies that we've acquired, let alone those we've passed on."

"I have all the presentations and data there; do you think that would be useful to Mitch?" Alia asked.

Shayla thought for a second or so and replied, "Let's do this. I'll have him join us at our one-on-one this Friday. I've been wanting you and Mitch to get to know one another more anyway. We can share with him what you have and engage him in a dialogue regarding what he needs. I need to get ahead of him on what he needs for myself and you. If that doesn't work, I'll talk to him directly about the best ways to get the data he needs." With that, Shayla stood up, thanked

Alia, and said, "I need to apologize to you more often!" Both smiled as Shayla left Alia's office.

Alia was so pleased and relieved with the outcome that she texted Whitney to let her know how things went.

Lesson learned - Even the best-prepared conversations won't go as planned, which is even more reason to be proactive.

CHAPTER 11
TCB with Sr. Leaders (C-Suite)

Alia had a meeting coming up later in the week with Clint Gaines, the company's General Counsel. She and Clint met regularly regarding language to add to the website, so she decided to work on framing a conversation she'd like to have with him that is unrelated to their scheduled meeting. Clint has begun to make "suggestions" about marketing related "look and feel" issues on the site. While Alia accepts feedback from all over the company regularly, Clint's suggestions feel more like "demands." And he was becoming more insistent.

As had become her practice before all critical conversations, Alia began by writing out key considerations.

- Clint and I work together extremely well in ensuring the company's intellectual property is well protected on the website. I want to protect that part of our relationship at all costs.

- Clint and I have worked together only sporadically with very specific task deliverables in the past. I've never had to have a conversation of any significance until now.

- While I could certainly suggest Clint talk to Shayla directly, I want to make sure Clint and I continue to work well together and that he sees me as a key resource. I also want to make sure that he understands the boundaries of our relationship.

Alia then completed framing her conversation with Clint.

Groundwork	Conversation Plan
Name: Clint Gaines	**Next Step:** Wait until right time arises organically
Position: C-Suite	
Situation: Senior leader overstepping their authority. Otherwise, great coworker and want to build relationship.	**Approach:** Set stage for great relationship
	Positional Impact: Heavy time & responsibility demands.
Objective: Clarify boundaries or rules of engagement	**Pace:** Focus on the facts, then move deliberately
Trust Level: Developing	
Comm. Driver: Precision	**Success Description:** Clint leaves conversation understanding my viewpoint without being offended.
Considerations: Political considerations – Clint is quite influential. I don't want to alienate him.	
	Opening: Clint, I'm glad you brought that up…

On Thursday morning, Clint and Alia completed a successful and productive meeting in Clint's office about changes to intellectual property language, when Clint brought up the inevitable.

"Hey, before you leave, Alia, I noticed the website still doesn't reflect the suggested changes around consulting services I brought up with you last week."

Alia could feel herself tensing up. She reviewed her conversation plan before meeting with Clint, as she thought he might surface this subject. "I'm glad you brought that up. We should discuss expectations around that. I see your suggestion on the consulting services as different than your wording changes around the company's IP statement," Alia said. (She then thought to herself, "Okay Alia, it's out there, you started with facts, that's good. Now go with it, make it productive, remember he has tons on his plate and has been a good partner in other ways.")

Clint replied, "Well yeah. They are different in that the changes in IP have to be made to protect us. I see the changes in the consulting services language helping to strengthen the IP language as well as having marketing appeal," Clint asserted confidently.

"Where I see the difference, and please let me know if we agree or not here, is that deciding the language and look and feel of materials around consulting services falls under my responsibility while the IP language falls directly under yours. So, I'm thinking your consulting services wording suggestion is just that, a suggestion. A good one that I'm considering, along with the other feedback I get from across the company. Now the IP language, that's all yours, as I see it. Am I off here?" Alia asked.

"Let me ask you a question, Alia, based on what you just said there," Clint said.

"Sure," Alia replied while she held her breath and tried not to show her nervousness.

"How many 'suggestions' do you get from others across the company from people who think they know marketing and what the website should look like in one way or another?" With this, Clint smiled.

"You have no idea, Clint. It's constant. And appreciated. Truly. Our employees have caught things on our site and made suggestions from other locations they've visited that we've implemented. That said, we receive far more suggestions for changes than we could ever implement, and of course people almost never agree on what they want in a site or in an online marketing campaign. There is a lot to be considered." ("Okay, I got a bit vulnerable there. Let's see how that's received... Alia thought to herself.)

"I get it. I probably drew outside the lines a bit. I'll back off. But I still think it's a great idea and it would help reinforce the IP language."

"Understood. I'll let you know, but no promises, okay?" Alia said with a smile.

"Understood. Alright, gotta run. See you next week, Alia."

"You too, Clint. Thanks again."

CHAPTER 12
TCB with Direct Reports

Alia and Whitney were visiting their parents and spending the weekend at their home just outside the city. After dinner, the sisters were sitting in their dad's study. Whitney was reading a book, while Alia was preparing for her weekly meeting with Darius Royston, one of her direct reports and the company's most senior Internet Marketing Coordinator. Alia interrupted her sister's solitude by saying, "Okay so I'm going to describe an issue I'm having with a direct report now."

"Out loud?" Whitney asked.

"We both know the answer to that," Alia continued. "I'm having an issue with my best Marketing Coordinator. Over the last few months, I've noticed that he's been pawning off parts of his job, particularly monitoring Search Engine Optimization (SEO), to other Coordinators in return for doing what he likes to do—customer marketing plan development. While from time to time that's okay, the intent of the team is to be comprised of full-service internet marketing professionals who can do everything our department offers. Darius has been with the company just shy of five years, with two years in his current role, and is the longest tenured employee on the team. Others naturally gravitate to his gregarious, friendly demeanor, abundant knowledge, and he is a natural leader on the team. He has expressed interest in the past in becoming a team lead. However, his inconsistent performance in this area keeps me from investing fully in that plan."

"Have you told him what you just told me?" Whitney asked.

"No. Not that clearly, at least not directly to him. I am clear about role expectations, and his trading off work does not fit with what I want. What I really want is for my team to be professional adults and do their jobs the way they know they should be done!"

"Whoa!" Whitney said, surprised by her sister's sudden level of irritation. "It looks like we may have paddled into deeper waters here." Both sisters laughed, and Alia explained, "Yeah, that hit a nerve. I know that in marketing, we have 'the rule of seven,' where a consumer needs to hear a message seven times before they take action to buy a product or service. As I think about it now, the same must hold true for messages to employees?" Alia asked.

"Absolutely! It helps to hear it in different forums and media as well. Given the fact that Darius has been in the role for a while now, it sounds like re-explaining the role boundaries, in other words, clarifying expectations, is in order." Whitney continued, "One of (if not the) most prevalent leadership styles I see at play in workplaces is one that no leader ever intends or would say is their preferred style - 'hinting and hoping.' You do not want to fall prey to that."

Alia said, "Wow. I haven't heard that phrase before, but I sure have seen it! Thanks, Whitney. That was helpful. Okay, you can go back to your book now," Alia said as her sister sighed and did just that.

As Monday of the new week came around, Alia was getting ready for her one-on-one meeting with Darius and reviewed her conversation plan before he arrived.

Groundwork	Conversation Plan
Name: Darius Royston	**Next Step:** Discuss during next regularly scheduled meeting
Position: Direct Report	
Situation: Darius is only doing the parts of job he enjoys most & leaving the aspects he doesn't like to others.	**Approach:** Set stage for great relationship
	Positional Impact: I have decision rights
Objective: Provide direction/set expectations	**Pace:** Cultivate & collaborate
Trust Level: Strong	**Success Description:** Have Darius understand the importance of completing all job responsibilities.
Comm. Driver: Relationships	
Considerations: While I trust Darius generally, his task avoidance in some performance areas give me pause in promoting him any time soon.	**Opening:** Darius, I'd like to have a conversation about the importance of your performing all the responsibilities of the Internet Marketing Coordinator position.

Darius joined her in her office, on time as always, and greeted her with a smile and a funny customer story that had just happened. When they got done discussing Darius' projects and what he needed from Alia, she was reminded of how autonomously Darius worked, and yet she always felt up to date and included. She was never surprised by anything going on in Darius' accounts, especially bad news. In fact, in the rare instances when there was bad news, she remembered Darius immediately bringing her up to date and problem-solving with her in advance.

When they were done, she used her opening phrase, "I'd like to have a conversation about the importance of your performing all of the responsibilities of the Internet Marketing Coordinator position."

"Oh great," Darius said. "I was hoping we could discuss this soon as well. Do you still need me to take the lead on all new customer marketing plans? I love it, as you know, but I'm getting way behind on the SEO stuff that my core customers need and it makes me feel that I don't have the whole picture in my relationship with them."

As Darius was talking, Alia remembered that she had given Darius the assignment of taking the lead on new customer marketing almost a year ago to reduce the impact on (then) two brand-new team members and Alia herself, as her time was almost entirely consumed with integrating new companies. She must have never communicated with him to that she wanted this to stop and was meant to be temporary. Was this possible?!?!

She paused and responded to Darius by saying, "Oh my Gosh, Darius. I never told you to go back to your 'normal' job, did I?!?!?!?"

"Was I supposed to?" Darius asked quizzically.

"No. I dropped the ball completely, and I'm so sorry. I never circled back with you to see how you were doing with that assignment, nor to discuss changes. Yes, going forward, let's get you back to having the full complement of responsibilities for your customers and shift customer marketing plan responsibilities to the other team members," Alia answered.

"No problem at all. In fact, if you'd like to make customer marketing planning my permanent—"

Alia then interrupted, "Nice try, Darius! Let's talk about what's next for you once I pick up the ball I dropped, next week during our one-on-one. I'll schedule a meeting with the team for Monday to clear things up."

"You got it!" Darius said enthusiastically.

CHAPTER 13
1+1 *and Putting It All Together*

Alia was shaken after her conversation with Darius. In her mind, she had been thinking he was shirking responsibilities for some time, when in fact, he was just following her wishes.

Alia wondered how many other assumptions she had made that she considered "facts." No sooner was she having that thought than one of her least favorite colleagues, Martin Skowron, a Sales Executive responsible for physical plant projects, called on her cell phone. She let the call go to voicemail and decided to head to lunch to see if she could change her luck.

As she headed to lunch, she ran right into Martin on her way out. In an annoyed tone, he said, "Did you listen to my voicemail?" Without waiting for an answer, he continued, "We have a problem that needs to be solved before I get on a plane Friday morning, Alia. When can you talk with me?"

"Martin, I'm totally booked this afternoon with meetings made weeks ago. Can we meet first thing tomorrow, Thursday morning?"

"If that's the best you can do, I have no choice." Martin was clearly frustrated.

"Send me all of the information you can on the situation and what you want from me, and I'll read it tonight and be ready to talk tomorrow," Alia assured him.

"That's fine. I'll do that Alia, but 'no' can't be an answer on this one. I don't think you realize how hard it is to get a sale in what I do. Come prepared to problem solve tomorrow." With that, Martin turned and walked away.

Alia lost her appetite after that interaction and decided to go for a walk instead to clear her head. As she walked, she was doing all she could to try to breathe and put the last couple of hours in perspective. After twenty minutes or so, she was feeling better and texted Whitney to see if she was available for dinner tonight to discuss the last week and as importantly, discuss the situations with Martin and Darius.

Whitney was available and the two sisters agreed to meet at Whitney's house, where Alia would buy and deliver dinner. Luckily, Alia's afternoon went better than her morning did. In fact, one of her afternoon meetings got canceled, giving her the time to come up to speed on the customer situation she and Martin would be discussing tomorrow. It also gave her an opportunity to complete The Conversation Blueprint template for her meeting with him and send it to Whitney before dinner.

Groundwork	Conversation Plan
Name: Martin Skowron	**Next Step:** Schedule 1-1 meeting
Position: Colleague	**Approach:** Guarded and open
Situation: Frustrated colleague – Martin wants to offer his client online access that we have not allowed in the past, due to security concerns.	**Positional Impact:** Neutral
	Pace: Get to the "bottom line" quickly
Objective: Solve business problem	**Success Description:** Share new process with Martin and see if this will satisfy his and the client's request.
Trust Level: Low/Weak	
Comm. Driver: Results	
Considerations: Past negative history makes me nervous to fully trust Martin. Martin's request will also require Clint's input.	**Opening:** Martin, I read all of what you sent and am ready to see what we can do to solve your client's issues.

1+1 AND PUTTING IT ALL TOGETHER

When Whitney and Alia met, Alia wasn't sure where to begin. She didn't have to worry much about that, as Whitney said, "Why don't you start by telling me how all of the conversations you planned for went and how you felt about the process?"

Alia was relieved to not be thinking about her day, and the Martin situation, and gave her sister the following rundown.

"Well, I will continue to use the process, no question about that! I felt far more prepared and confident before talking to each, very different, person with each unique situation. The results speak for themselves, even when the results included learning things about myself that I didn't particularly like. With Cody, it felt so good to have it be okay to let myself be a friend and a team leader who relied on his ability to successfully lead his team. For the first time, I truly listened for understanding, and I think —well, I know—that we both got a great deal out of the conversation. I was far more able to identify areas where I thought Cody could improve that felt more like lifelines for him than criticisms. Things aren't where they need to be yet, but he has taken the first steps with his team, and initial indications are very positive.

The conversation with Shayla did not go as planned—not initially, anyway! I did complete the TCB template; however, she came into my office a couple of days before our one-on-one meeting to apologize for being short with me. Then what ensued was truly another 'great conversation.' At that point I was 'two for two!'" Alia laughed, using a baseball analogy.

"Did having the conversation before you intended throw you off?" Whitney asked.

"Not really. I realized we were going to have the conversation right then and there and I immediately focused on the crux of the desired outcome 'get on the table what she needs from me and let her share what's changed for her.' From there, things flowed naturally. I reviewed the template afterward and saw that we covered what I thought we needed to, and much more. After this conversation and the one with Cody, I felt that what most improved was my ability to listen.

Perhaps the process was forcing me to listen, but either way I don't care, provided that continues," Alia stated.

"I think pre-planning and imagining positive outcomes helps in everything we do. The results were all due to your hard work and abilities," Whitney offered.

Alia continued, "With Clint, I let the situation emerge organically. If he brought up his 'suggestions' again, which he did, I was prepared to engage in dialogue. I felt both confident and terrified in clarifying boundaries with Clint, as his style and mine are different, and his intelligence and position really intimidated me. He accepted the message well, though, and let me know he understood, in his own Clint way. I got the feeling our relationship went up a notch in his eyes with how I handled the situation."

"Sounds like three for three from where I sit!" Whitney offered jokingly.

Alia replied, "Agreed. Then my 'batting average' took a hit. With Darius, I was ready to discuss a need for a change in behavior. I was ready to let him know that I needed him to complete all aspects of his job, not only those he enjoyed. As I brought up the conversation, he was relieved and reminded me that I had asked him to take on the responsibilities he had taken from others and was glad to get back to helping his customer base fully. I totally forgot about that, Whit. He was one hundred percent right! I pivoted and panicked a bit, in my mind anyway, and ended the conversation early to give myself a chance to regroup. Three for four." With that, Alia waited for a response from her sister.

"Well, I'd argue you are four for four." After noticing a confused look on her sister's face, she continued, "You were able to get information you didn't have, and surface a false assumption on your part, even if that wasn't your intention. If you go back and look at the TCB template you completed for Darius, I'll bet a few of your answers would change."

"They did. I went back and changed them already. I couldn't stand having false information out there. What I worry about is how I went for so long with the wrong idea to begin with," Alia said.

Whitney then offered, "Part of what I hope is accomplished through The Conversation Blueprint process is the surfacing of assumptions to get to a more accurate picture of what our own contributions have been to the situations we face, in just this way. Even you must know you can't be perfect when it comes to leading others when you have such a demanding job that moves at such a fast pace. That's what good communication tools and processes are for. In this case, you really caught the situation before you acted on your incorrect assumptions. I'd call that a win every time."

"That's all very true. I feel better and get it now. Lesson learned. I'll need a little time to make sure that I remind myself that I was misperceiving the situation with Darius, because I held on to my inaccurate, or at least incomplete, views for a while and they started to shape how I viewed him."

"That's a great next step. Now what about this Martin character you told me about?" Whitney asked.

"Ah yes. Martin Skowron. We started at the company on the same day, and to be honest, I find his behavior to be obnoxious and rude most of the time. He is in sales and has a demanding job, but often approaches others in the company as if they work for him, and his priorities should always take precedence over whatever else anyone may be doing," Alia explained.

"Tell me how you really feel?" Whitney said.

"I know. I just mean that I don't really have a goal of having a close relationship with Martin. If I'm honest, it's not really that important to me to have anything more than we have now," Alia admitted.

"Before you go there, let me just ask what assumptions you may be making about Martin and his intentions?" Whitney asked.

"What are you driving at? Can you just let me know what to do on this one? Any more self-reflection today and I may seriously lose it," Alia confided.

"Sure thing. Let's look at your opening statement for Martin." With that, Whitney referred to the template Alia completed for Martin. She also brought up the openings for Shayla and Cody.

> **Martin Opening:** "Martin, I read all of what you sent and am ready to see what we can do to solve your client's issues."
>
> **Cody Opening:** "Thanks for making the time to talk. I wanted to finish the conversation we had in my office last week. I was pressed for time and didn't feel like I listened too well."
>
> **Shayla Opening:** "I want to bring up our last conversation when you were looking for the search data on our consulting services. I didn't feel like you got what you needed from me."

"Let's see what we notice when we compare your openings for Martin, Cody, and Shayla," Whitney asked.

Alia and Whitney read and re-read the statements. Seeing them side by side allowed the sisters to get an interesting perspective and insight into Alia's way of approaching her recent conversations.

"I'll go first," Alia said. "It's not even so much what I see. It's more how I feel when I read them. I really wanted to have conversations with Cody and Shayla, and I really don't want to with Martin. That feeling comes through in the language I chose for the different openings, loudly and clearly. The language with Martin is so stiff and uncaring whereas with Cody and Shayla, the words are much more welcoming."

"Great pick up," Whitney said. "Okay if I add what I see?"

"Absolutely," Alia said, now more into the exercise and conversation than ever.

"You seem far more curious and open to exploring with Shayla and Cody, whereas with Martin, you start with a conclusion. Now, Martin is someone interested in results, so I'm not suggesting this is bad in any way, but I do know that it is hard to surface any underlying assumptions if we start with conclusions," Whitney said.

"Well, how do I do that with someone with whom I don't have much trust, and whose relationship is as hit or miss as Martin's and mine is?" Alia wondered.

"Curiosity and questions go hand in hand," Whitney offered. "Can you think of a way to show Martin that you are serious about his issue while also inquiring into whether you truly are addressing what's most important to him?"

Alia tried the following. "Martin, I read all of what you sent and am ready to see what we can do to solve your client's issues. I realized though that I may not know what a 'fully successful outcome' of this situation really means for you. Do you mind if we start with that and then get into problem-solving mode?"

Whitney nodded her approval.

"Even if I don't love Martin, improving our relationship only helps the company, my team, and the two of us," Alia added.

"If you can hang in a bit longer, let's look at Darius' opening just to see if we can learn anything there." With that, Whitney brought up Alia's opening for her conversation with Darius.

> "Darius, I'd like to have a conversation about the importance of your performing all of the responsibilities of the Internet Marketing Coordinator position."

"Wow," Alia was surprised at how stiff and formal the opening now seemed. "It looks just like the opening for Martin. No curiosity. No caring. I can see my past assumptions and state of mind reflected in my words," Alia said.

Whitney then asked her sister if she remembered the conversation they had about the theory of contribution. Alia let her know she did. Whitney then went on to write "1 + 1" on a napkin. She said, "In relationships we control what we say (1) and do, just as the other person controls what they say and do (1), but we also influence the '+' and therefore have more than 50% say in the final 'sum' of the interaction. Let me give you an example. My mentor Chris and I were having difficulty communicating well at one point in our relationship at work and it really bothered me. I decided to go into our next conversation assuming that Chris was speaking and listening with positive intent—that is, he was only saying things that he felt were to my benefit. At the time, I was not listening with positive intent. In fact, while preparing for our next conversation, I could identify where I had been defensive. Our next conversation was indeed a great one. I controlled both what I said and did, as did Chris, but I also influenced the '+' by responding non-defensively to Chris, and thus he responded in kind. The 'sum' of that conversation equaled way more than its parts."

Alia looked at her sister and said, "Where did you come from? I can recall SEVERAL instances from our childhood, where this person that I'm talking to now, was NOWHERE to be found!"

"She's still absent at times, believe me!" Whitney said.

"Seriously, Whit. Thank you. This makes a ton of sense and has helped me a lot," Alia said. She then revised the template based on the conversation she and Whitney had just completed.

CHAPTER 14
TCB with Difficult Colleagues

Groundwork

Name: Martin Skowron
Position: Colleague
Situation: Frustrated colleague – Martin wants to offer his client online access that we have not allowed in the past, due to security concerns.
Objective: Solve business problem
Trust Level: Low/Weak
Comm. Driver: Results
Considerations: Past negative history makes me nervous to fully trust Martin. Martin's request will likely also require Clint's input at some point, so understanding Martin's needs more clearly will help as we go further down this road.

Conversation Plan

Next Step: Schedule 1-1 meeting
Approach: Guarded and open
Positional Impact: Neutral
Pace: Get to the "bottom line" quickly
Success Description: Learn Martin and the client's needs and see if a new process being developed with Clint will satisfy the request.
Opening: Martin, I read what you sent and I'm ready to see what we can do to solve your client's issues. I realized though that I may not know what a 'fully successful outcome' of this situation really means for you. Do you mind if we start with that and then get into problem-solving mode?

The next morning, it was time to talk with Martin. Alia felt better about the possibility of having a productive conversation with Martin, but it was in no way a sure thing. Yesterday, Martin came in "hot" and Alia was expecting him to act similarly today.

Martin arrived at Alia's office. After she invited him in to sit down, and they exchanged "good morning" greetings, Martin began the conversation. "Well, did you read what I sent?"

"I did get a chance to read it all. Thanks for that. I'm ready to see what we can do to solve your client's issues. I realized though, that I may not know what a 'fully successful outcome' of this situation really means for you. Do you mind if we start with that and then get into problem-solving mode?" Alia said.

"My desired outcome is the same as the client's. They want access to some of the information that we make available to employees around building materials and suppliers. There's nothing proprietary to it that I see, we just happen to have a great system of finding and categorizing this information. My client is not a competitor in our space in any way," Martin replied, still a bit irritated in his tone, but the irritation tailed off a bit as he concluded, as if perhaps in hearing what he wanted out loud, he may have "heard" why others may object to the idea.

"So, if I hear you right, the client's real need is to have quicker access to the information in our system. This would help them identify the suppliers and materials we share in our businesses, but not as a competitor. Do I have that right?" Alia said.

"Yes. That's basically it. The better our client does, the more they'll work with us. I don't know why we don't offer this anyway as a perk to clients," Martin replied.

Alia continued with her clarifying questions and was now engaged in problem solving and curious as to whether there may be an opportunity here. "In your e-mail, you mentioned the client wanted to sign-in to our system directly for access to that software. Would there be another solution they may be satisfied with that could get them their information quickly, without allowing direct access?" Alia asked.

Martin replied, "It's the direct access that's the issue, isn't it? The software is stand alone and they wouldn't have access to anything else in the system."

"Do you know that for sure, Martin? I'm not so sure about that, and I'm thinking to someone like Clint Gaines' ear, that asking for on-line access to any proprietary system may be a hard no. I have an idea. Can I float something by you?" Alia asked.

"I guess, but I can already tell I'm not getting what I need." Martin crossed his arms and sighed as he finished.

Alia thought to herself, "Martin, throw me a bone here?!?! My goodness, can't you see the obstacles ahead of you and that I'm trying to find a way to help you?" She paused and formed her proposed solution in her head for a second before continuing. "Martin, what if we partnered your client with a direct line to a Marketing Coordinator for the requests that require system access?"

Martin paused for a second and said, "Go on. How would that work?"

"Well, right now what your client wants is not in their, or any client's contract, correct?" Alia asked.

"Yeah, that's right," Martin said.

"Well, what if we amended the contract to add that service, and allowed your client access to a Marketing Coordinator who could verify that requests meet contractual guidelines and looks up the information for the client in real-time?" Alia replied.

"Can we do that?" Martin asked.

"We'd have to get Clint involved, but I think this has a much better chance of being approved," Alia said.

"If we did add this to the contract, we could come up with a fee arrangement for the service. As we're talking, I am seeing the value it could bring to this and other clients. How fast could we make this happen do you think?" Martin asked.

"We can see how quickly Clint could meet with us if you want. On my end, I could partner your client with a Marketing Coordinator easily, provided there are contractual guidelines in place. What do you think?" Alia asked.

"I still want what I asked for and think we could allow limited access to clients without there being a risk. Clint Gaines is a tougher sell than you, and I don't see him giving in to anything he sees as a risk. My experience with him has been that he thinks in a binary 'yes/no' way. I think I could sell the client on your proposed option. Do you think Clint will buy it?" Martin asked.

"I don't know. There's one way to find out. I'm okay with doing this Martin, even though it will cause some extra work in my team. That may sway Clint."

"Let's get a meeting with him. Thanks Alia," Martin said.

"You're welcome, Martin," she said with a smile.

With that, they scheduled the meeting with Clint for later that afternoon. Alia left the conversation with Martin exhausted, but satisfied. She knew Martin wasn't "thrilled" with their conversation, but she felt she did her absolute best to help him, protect the company, and potentially even find a new service for clients.

CHAPTER 15
New Build's New Sr. Leader

Alia had the conversation with Martin and Clint. She played a key role in brokering a solution with which she, Martin, and Clint could accept, and ultimately met the client's needs.

Martin and Alia may never be in one another's inner circles, however the trust and respect between them is better than it has ever been. That is certainly something to celebrate.

Alia continued to work hard at building relationships and using the TCB process for the most important relationships and conversations she encountered. In fact, this became second nature, because it worked for her. When things work, we tend to use them and tell others about them, which is exactly what Alia did. She even adapted the tool when dealing with two or more employees and the teams she led.

Over the next year, Alia's relationships flourished, and her technical and leadership expertise grew to the point where she was promoted to a position reporting directly to NewBuild's CEO, upon Shayla's deciding to leave NewBuild to work at a smaller firm that reminded her of NewBuild from years past. Alia is now a direct colleague of Clint's and continues to enjoy a strong relationship with him.

Darius was elevated to Alia's role and was welcomed by the team as the obvious choice for promotion. Darius and Cody now have Alia as their direct leader. While it was strange for Cody and Alia at first, they have both learned to embrace their relationship inside and outside of the organization.

Alia has kept in constant contact with Whitney, who continues to do the work that she loves, can't imagine ever retiring from, and plans to continue doing for the rest of her life.

EPILOGUE
Putting TCB into Practice

Leaders at all levels must take responsibility for building and maintaining strong relationships at every turn. So often our other responsibilities come at us so quickly that it becomes easy to forget how important other people are to our immediate and enduring success.

In writing this book, I did a great deal of thinking about the act of conversing, and it struck me more than ever how important the speaker's role is in being thoughtful and intentional before engaging in dialogue. For it is only the speaker who truly knows the messages they intend to send. In thinking back on my own conversations that went sideways, it is almost always those where I put little (or no) thought into what I was saying.

I use TCB to plan for my own successful conversations. The process forces me to slow down and focus on what's truly important. I rarely, if ever, come up with my final desired outcome on the first try. Like with so many things, repeating the fundamentals of having great conversations leads to a deeper understanding of the factors that bring about the outcomes we desire. In this way, the process also becomes second nature and allows us to apply the practices of TCB and improve the outcomes of unplanned and emergent conversations as well. Focusing, for example, on a new colleague's need to be precise and getting things right the first time, lets us know that we would be well suited to provide the data and rationale to support our conclusions in advance of key conversations when possible—or even stop a first conversation that is underway, to provide this information and pick up the conversation later.

The importance of being self-aware came up as a common theme shared among the best communicators. Knowing our own preferences, strengths, and how we're feeling during conversations goes a long way to being able to recognize and help develop these same traits in others. After using TCB for some time, I noticed my own preferences, strengths, and shortcomings as a communicator. For example, the conversation between Whitney and Alia, where Alia realizes that the language she is using for some conversations is very stiff and unfeeling, came from personal experience in using TCB over time.

The intent of writing The Conversation Blueprint was to help others have and enjoy the benefits of great conversations. Visit both www.taddwyer.com and www.theconversationblueprint.com for all things TCB. I invite you to share your stories and examples of great conversations with me, to keep the learning presented in the book alive.

Thanks so much for reading and keep the great conversations flowing!

ACKNOWLEDGEMENTS

Thanks to Gary Oshiro for being the first person to read the book and provide pivotal feedback that materially improved the story and made the book more readable for those to follow. His consistent interest in the project, subject matter expertise, friendship, and counsel are things for which I will be forever grateful.

I want to acknowledge John Feriancek, Joelle Marquis, and Nick Saccaro, for taking time out of their intensely busy executive careers and reading the book as content experts and providing great advice on context and story flow. Along with Gary, their input and guidance were instrumental in making the book you just read more enjoyable and substantive.

Thanks to Curt Graves, both for being the inspiration behind the Clint Gaines character, and for being one of the first people, along with my wife, to see the outline of the book and provide excellent, immediate feedback.

Undying gratitude to my mom Tina, and my sister Lesley, for being my first role models of what it takes to live and lead by example, particularly through difficult times.

Special thanks to Carole Fredericks, my first true mentor who taught me so much about organization development and what it means to truly lead.

I want to thank the leaders and clients who I've had the pleasure of serving and learning from. Without you, this book would not have been possible.

Thanks to my friends and family for their belief in me and constant support and encouragement.

ABOUT THE AUTHOR

Tad Dwyer is an organization development consultant and leadership coach, with significant experience in developing and implementing strategic and large-scale culture change initiatives, particularly for portfolio companies of private equity owned businesses. As a coach, he uses a needs-based approach to identify client wins based on their skills and abilities, and the unique situations they face.

Prior to founding his consulting practice, Tad held senior training, development, and leadership positions in the banking and insurance industries as well as in portfolio companies owned by Arsenal Capital Partners. He holds a master's degree in Organization and Management from Antioch New England Graduate School, where he also served for several years as an Associate Core faculty member.

Tad and his family reside in beautiful Denver, Colorado but will always call southern New Hampshire home.